W9-CCC-637

5 0508 01700 450 9

j 973.3 Mae 2005
Maestro, Betsy.
Liberty or death

11/05

Liberty or Death

The American Revolution ★ 1763–1783

by **Betsy Maestro**

illustrated by **Giulio Maestro**

▰HarperCollins*Publishers*

Hamilton East Public Library
One Library Plaza
Noblesville, IN 46060

Liberty or Death: The American Revolution, 1763–1783

Text copyright © 2005 by Betsy Maestro Illustrations copyright © 2005 by Giulio Maestro

Manufactured in China. All rights reserved. No part of this book may be used or reproduced in any manner
whatsoever without written permission except in the case of brief quotations embodied in critical articles and reviews. For information
address HarperCollins Children's Books, a division of HarperCollins Publishers, 1350 Avenue of the Americas, New York, NY 10019.
www.harperchildrens.com

Library of Congress Cataloging-in-Publication Data

Maestro, Betsy.

Liberty or death : the American Revolution, 1763-1783 / by Betsy Maestro ; illustrated by Giulio Maestro.

p. cm.

ISBN 0-688-08802-3 — ISBN 0-688-08803-1 (lib. bdg.)

1. United States—History—Revolution, 1775-1783—Juvenile literature. 2. United States—History—Revolution, 1775-1783—Causes—
Juvenile literature. [1. United States—History—Revolution, 1775-1783.] I. Maestro, Giulio, ill. II. Title.

E208 .M3 2005

973.3–dc21   00-054042
                                                                                                                                                                             CIP
                                                                                                                                                                             AC

1 2 3 4 5 6 7 8 9 10   ❖   First Edition

In the year 1763, the French and Indian Wars came to an end. For more than seventy years, France and England had fought for control of the land and riches of North America. The Spanish had settlements in the Southwest and Florida but had left the French and English, along with their Indian allies, to battle it out for the rest of the vast continent. In the end, the English were victorious. As part of the peace agreement, England gained most of New France as well as Spanish Florida. So in 1763, English territory in North America stretched from Canada to Florida and from the Atlantic Ocean to the Mississippi River.

Although the war with France had ended, England's troubles in America were far from over. Indian tribes faithful to the French rebelled against British rule. But the military might of the British soldiers and the colonial militia proved overwhelming, and the short-lived Indian revolution failed. Now, however, the stirrings of a very different revolution began to rumble throughout the thirteen English colonies.

CANADA

Mississippi River

THE 13 COLONIES

ATLANTIC OCEAN

FLORIDA

ENGLISH TERRITORY AFTER 1763

A tax stamp for licenses and legal papers

King George III

Colonial teapot from around 1765

Seventy years of fighting cost Great Britain a great deal of money, and now they expected the colonists to pay back some of this cost. So the British began to tax their subjects in America. The American colonists were used to ignoring unwanted interference from their mother country, but now England was determined to enforce the law. The new Stamp Act of 1765 said that all official papers sold in the colonies, such as newspapers and licenses, had to have a British stamp attached to them. Naturally, the stamps had to be purchased from a British official. The colonists were furious!

In Boston and New York, groups of concerned Americans, called patriots, organized public demonstrations against the Stamp Act. Protest leaders like Sam Adams and James Otis of Massachusetts stirred the crowds with angry speeches. In Virginia, Patrick Henry echoed their cry—Great Britain had no right to tax American colonists without their consent. Throughout the colonies the idea took hold: no taxation without representation!

Colonists hang a dummy of a British tax collector to protest the Stamp Act

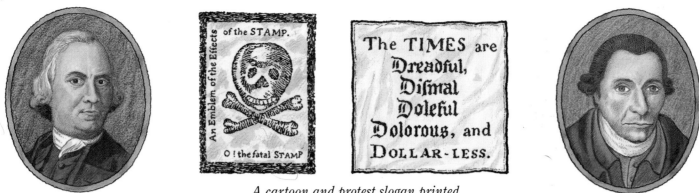

Sam Adams

A cartoon and protest slogan printed in a newspaper in 1765

Patrick Henry

In October 1765, delegates from nine colonies met in New York City to talk about the Stamp Act. They all agreed it was unfair and sent petitions to England. Many citizens and business owners simply refused to use the stamps. Finally, the British government gave in and removed the tax. But less than two years later, the colonists were ordered to pay new taxes on paper, glass, and tea. As a protest, they boycotted English goods. If they didn't buy the goods, they wouldn't have to pay the taxes. When public rallies in Boston became unruly, armed British soldiers, called regulars, were sent in to keep order. But the sight of so many red uniforms made the colonists even angrier.

Angry New York merchants decide to boycott British goods

In Boston, on the night of March 5, 1770, what began with name-calling between a British soldier and a colonist grew into a violent clash that stunned the city. A disorderly crowd gathered outside the Customs House and the soldier called for help. More soldiers arrived, but by then a mob of hundreds was shouting threats and throwing snowballs. The frightened soldiers were pushed and shoved, and one soldier was hit with a club. The soldiers responded by firing their muskets into the crowd. People fled in all directions, but five colonists were left dead or dying, including Crispus Attucks, a black sailor. Patriot groups, like the Sons of Liberty, used this event to rile up the citizenry by calling what had happened the Boston Massacre.

The Boston Massacre

The Boston Tea Party

The British realized that their problems in America were more serious than they had first thought. They canceled most of the new taxes, and life in the colonies settled into an uneasy peace. The only remaining tax was on British tea. The colonists got around this tax by drinking Dutch tea. But when British ships blocked shipments of Dutch tea into Boston, the colonists announced that they would not allow British tea to be unloaded in their harbor either. On the night of December 16, 1773, patriots, disguised as Indians, boarded the tea ships in the harbor. They cut open three hundred and forty-two chests of tea, worth thousands of British pounds, and dumped them into the sea. The Boston Tea Party, as it was called, infuriated King George III and Parliament. They punished the citizens of Massachusetts by closing the port of Boston. They stripped the Massachusetts government of its power, banned town meetings, and forced ordinary families to house British soldiers.

These "Intolerable Acts" brought immediate calls for action against British rule. Citizens throughout the thirteen colonies rallied to support the people of Massachusetts. On September 5, 1774, the First Continental Congress met in Philadelphia. Forty-five delegates from twelve colonies gathered to decide what to do next. Some delegates, like Sam Adams and Patrick Henry, were considered radicals because they were ready to fight the British immediately. Henry shouted that he was "not a Virginian but an American." But others, like John Jay from New York, were more conservative and wanted to find a peaceful compromise with England. Still other delegates, like John Adams and George Washington, listened to both sides and carefully considered all the possibilities.

The First Continental Congress met in Carpenter's Hall in Philadelphia

Massachusetts minuteman

General Thomas Gage

Congress sent a list of complaints to the British government and planned a boycott of all English goods throughout the colonies. The delegates returned home to organize militias in each town, city, and county—volunteer fighting units, ready to march and defend the colonies if and when needed.

Some were called minutemen because they could respond instantly to any emergency. Leaders of the other colonies agreed to unite and stand with Massachusetts if the British moved against them. The people of Massachusetts were worried—no one knew what would happen next.

The British appointed General Thomas Gage as commander of all the British troops in North America. He arrived in Boston to take charge of about four thousand soldiers and four warships anchored in the harbor. But Gage would need a bigger army because the colonial militias were growing larger each day. Thousands of ordinary citizens were willing to take up arms for the patriot cause.

British regular

British warships in Boston Harbor

In March of 1775, Patrick Henry delivered a speech to the colonial legislature in Virginia. In his forceful voice, he said that the time for talking was past and that the colonies must be ready to fight for freedom. His powerful words convinced many listeners, including George Washington and Thomas Jefferson, to support his plan to raise and train a militia. "I know not what course others may take," Henry said, "but as for me, give me liberty or give me death!"

Patrick Henry addressing the Virginia legislature

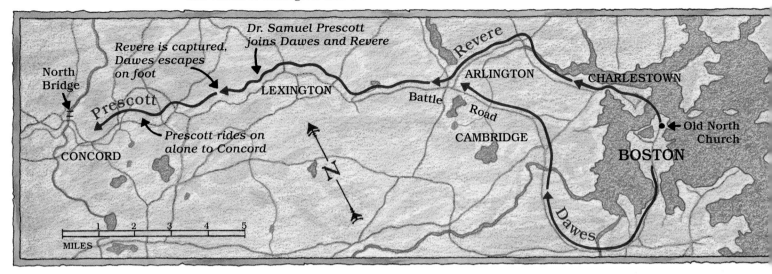

The routes to Lexington and Concord in Massachusetts

Meanwhile, the situation in Massachusetts grew worse every day. British troops were on the move, and colonial leaders readied for war. General Gage received orders to arrest Sam Adams and John Hancock, the two organizers most wanted by the British. Gage planned a secret march to Concord to seize weapons stored there by the colonists. But word of the plan leaked out, and on April 18, patriot spies learned that the British were setting out for Concord that very night. Word was sent to Paul Revere and William Dawes, who agreed to ride out to warn Adams and Hancock, who were hiding in Lexington, a town near Concord. As part of a prearranged plan, Revere asked a fellow patriot to hang two lanterns in the tower of Old North Church to signal that the British were traveling across the bay by boat rather than coming by land across Boston Neck. Revere and Dawes mounted their horses to ride north toward Lexington and Concord, taking two different routes. In towns along the way, they shouted their warning to all who could hear: "The regulars are coming out!" Hearing that British troops were on the way, local volunteers grabbed their guns and began to assemble.

Paul Revere

Toward morning, on April 19, 1775, as British soldiers approached Lexington, about one hundred militiamen, including many minutemen, gathered on the village green with their leader, Captain John Parker. The men didn't intend to fire at the redcoats, only to hold their ground to keep the British from advancing. A British officer rode forward and ordered them to disband. As they backed off, a shot was fired. The British soldiers were ordered to fire, and a volley of shots rang out. Eight patriots lay dead.

In just minutes, the Battle of Lexington was over. No one knows who fired that first shot—"the shot heard round the world." But it was the first shot fired in battle in the American Revolution. The Battle of Lexington began a long day of skirmishes between the British and the Americans. As the British marched on to Concord to carry out their orders, small groups of minutemen engaged the redcoats many times, firing their muskets and then withdrawing. The British were forced to abandon their mission, and they slowly began to retreat toward Boston.

The Battle of Lexington

Patriots turn back the British at Concord's North Bridge

Patriots turn back the British at Concord's North Bridge

All along the way patriots fired at them from the cover of barns and trees. As more and more militiamen arrived, the redcoats were under attack at every turn. They were greatly relieved to meet reinforcements as they neared Lexington. There, the frustrated British raided and burned some houses, killing the men and boys inside. By nightfall, the exhausted British regulars at last reached the safety of their encampment near Boston. Although the Americans had lost almost fifty men, they felt victorious. They had held their ground against the well-trained British soldiers. Volunteer militia began arriving from nearby states to help Massachusetts. The combined forces soon numbered almost twenty thousand men. But to mount a true defense against the well-armed British, the colonists would need more than just muskets and rifles.

The British retreat under fire

Lake Champlain

Crown Point

Ticonderoga

Lake George

(later Vermont)

Conn. R.

NEW HAMPSHIRE

PART OF MASSACHUSETTS (later Maine)

NEW YORK

Hudson River

Boston

MASSACHUSETTS

CONNECTICUT

RHODE ISLAND

New York

NEW JERSEY

Benedict Arnold

Ethan Allen

When spies reported that the British-held Fort Ticonderoga in New York was not well defended, the Americans hatched a plan to capture its large arsenal.

Under the command of Captain Benedict Arnold of Connecticut and Ethan Allen of Vermont, colonial forces seized the fort and all its artillery. But how would they get the heavy weapons to Boston?

In May of 1775, the Second Continental Congress met in Philadelphia. Although the delegates were disturbed by the news of the bloodshed in Massachusetts, most were not ready to take up arms against the British. For almost two months they argued about which path to follow. Some members still thought a peaceful solution was possible. But Benjamin Franklin, just back from England, reported that his efforts at peace talks had failed.

So Congress decided to choose a leader for an army made up of joint forces from all of the colonies. When John Adams proposed a highly respected Virginian for the job, the final vote was unanimous: Colonel George Washington would be the commander in chief of the newly formed Continental Army. As Washington left for Massachusetts to take charge of his troops, three new British generals arrived in Boston.

George Washington

William Howe

William Howe, Henry Clinton, and John Burgoyne began to plan a major campaign against the patriots. But before the British could organize, General Israel Putnam and Colonel William Prescott led more than a thousand colonial soldiers to a hilltop in Charlestown, across the river from Boston. Although they planned to fortify Bunker Hill, Breed's Hill was closer to the harbor. During the night of June 16, the men built an earthen fort surrounded by a ditch. In the morning, a surprised General Howe scrambled to ferry his troops across the bay on barges, protected by fire from British ships.

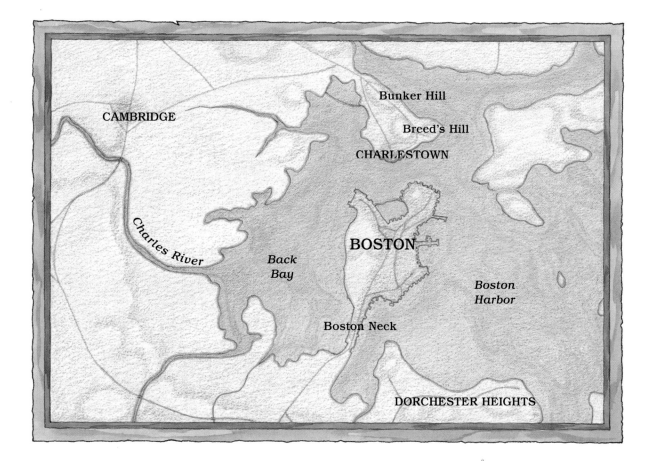

The battle on Breed's Hill

As Howe's men marched up the hill in neat formation, the Americans held their fire until they could see "the whites of their eyes," as they had been instructed. Showers of musket balls rained upon the British soldiers, and many fell. But at the third assault on the hill, the Americans ran out of ammunition and were forced to escape or be killed. In about ninety minutes, the Battle of Bunker Hill, as it came to be known, was over. It was a victory for the British, but at great human cost. Out of more than two thousand soldiers, there were at least two hundred dead and almost nine hundred wounded.

When news of the battle reached England, the British were furious. The colonies were in open rebellion, and if war was what they wanted, war was just what they would get!

Some members of Congress now wanted to approve a formal declaration of independence. But many delegates were still not ready to take such serious action. However, Congress did approve more money for the army, and they appointed officers to serve under Washington. They chose Artemus Ward, Israel Putnam, Philip Schuyler, and two retired British officers—Charles Lee and Horatio Gates.

When Washington reached Cambridge, near Boston, in July 1775, to take command of the army, he saw that he had a near-impossible task ahead of him. Ammunition and supplies were very low, and the Continental Army was made up of untrained soldiers not used to taking orders or following rules. Somehow Washington had to prepare these men for real warfare against experienced, professional soldiers. He also needed a bigger army, because the British were sending thousands of additional troops to North America.

Pennsylvania

Massachusetts

Rhode Island

Connecticut

Virginia

Maryland

Maryland, Virginia, and Pennsylvania sent companies of riflemen to join the Continental Army in Massachusetts. In addition to his six thousand soldiers, Washington had about ten thousand part-time men he could call on to fight when necessary. But these local militiamen had families, farms, and businesses to tend to. They couldn't always be there when needed and didn't always obey orders. Washington could do little but wait and hope that his standing army would stay the course. But some had already left for home, and as the year 1775 ended, prospects for the Continental Army looked very bleak indeed.

Early in January, however, everyone's spirits were lifted by the words of Thomas Paine, a strong supporter of the patriot cause. In a pamphlet called "Common Sense," Paine wrote that the iron rule of the British government should be answered by armed rebellion and a struggle for complete independence. "The sun never shined on a cause of greater worth," he said. "A government of our own is our natural right." Thousands of the pamphlets were sent out and read, and Paine's words rallied Americans to the cause.

Thomas Paine

COMMON SENSE:
ADDRESSED TO THE
INHABITANTS
OF
AMERICA,
On the following interesting
SUBJECTS.

I. Of the Origin and Design of Government in general, with concise Remarks on the English Constitution.
II. Of Monarchy and Hereditary Succession.
III. Thoughts on the present State of American Affairs.
IV. Of the present Ability of America, with some miscellaneous Reflections.

Written by an ENGLISHMAN.

Hauling the artillery from Fort Ticonderoga to Boston

A few weeks later, the Continental Army got wonderful news—the artillery from Fort Ticonderoga had arrived! Colonel Henry Knox, named as Washington's new commander of artillery, had produced a miracle. More than forty cannon and mortars, some weighing a ton each, had been dragged three hundred miles on sleds, pulled by one hundred and sixty oxen, through the snow and ice.

During the night of March 4, 1776, Washington sent more than two thousand of his troops on to Dorchester Heights, overlooking Boston Harbor. By morning, fortifications were built and the heavy artillery from Ticonderoga had been assembled and aimed at the British below.

The fortifications atop Dorchester Heights

It seemed to the British that only a huge army—maybe twenty thousand men—could have accomplished such a feat so quickly. So General Howe made a deal with Washington. His troops would leave Boston peacefully if they could go in complete safety. The British occupation of Boston was over. Some nine thousand British soldiers sailed for Halifax, Nova Scotia, along with more than a thousand Loyalists, colonial citizens who were still faithful to the king. With Massachusetts out of immediate danger, Washington and the Continental Army headed for New York, a Loyalist stronghold.

That May in Philadelphia, Congress was greatly cheered by news of the British withdrawal from Boston. They hoped for similar success in British-controlled Canada, and sent a large number of colonial soldiers north on this mission. Although no battles were won, the northern army kept the British busy, and stalled their march south, giving Washington much-needed time to build his forces.

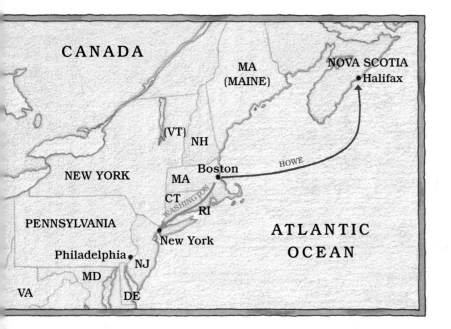

20

Benjamin Franklin

Thomas Jefferson

John Adams

Roger Sherman

Robert Livingston

Congress again turned their attention to the question of independence. Should the colonies fight for total independence from Britain? Were they really ready to completely break away from their mother country? Men like Richard Henry Lee of Virginia and John Adams argued yes, while others like John Dickinson of Pennsylvania and John Jay were still very much opposed. During this debate, shocking news arrived from England. Smuggled documents showed that the British had hired eighteen thousand paid German soldiers to help them in their fight against the colonists.

Almost immediately, Congress voted to declare independence from Great Britain. Benjamin Franklin, Thomas Jefferson, John Adams, Roger Sherman of Connecticut, and Robert Livingston of New York were asked to write a formal statement to send to the British government.

Congress met at the Pennsylvania Statehouse

Benjamin Franklin, John Adams, and Thomas Jefferson discuss the wording for the Declaration of Independence

Thomas Jefferson was chosen to do most of the writing, using ideas from all the members. He spent two weeks writing and revising many versions of the declaration before he felt the words were just right. While Jefferson worked, Congress heard that General Howe had arrived in New York with more than a hundred British ships! Now there was no doubt—the British were preparing for all-out war against the American colonies.

On June 28, Jefferson presented the final draft to Congress for debate. Everyone on both sides spoke with great emotion as they realized the importance of what they were about to do. At the first vote, only nine colonies approved the declaration. Some delegates were still uncertain about the course they were taking. But on July 2, when the final vote was taken, only New York remained undecided. Twelve colonies voted to declare their independence from England.

On July 4, 1776, the final version of the declaration was approved, and John Hancock, as president of Congress, signed the document on the spot. A signature on such a paper was treason—a betrayal of England, and a crime punishable by death. The other members of Congress would sign at a later date. The Declaration of Independence proclaimed that "all men are created equal" and that all people had the right to "life, liberty, and the pursuit of happiness." It said that citizens could change or throw out any government that did not allow its people to enjoy those rights. On July 15, the New York delegates added their vote, and made the decision to declare independence unanimous.

John Hancock

Hancock's famous signature

The final version of the declaration is presented to Congress

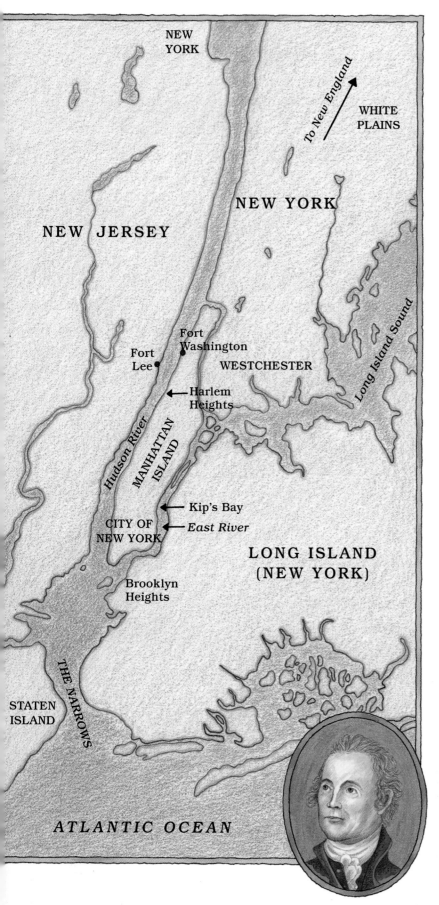

NEW
YORK

To New England

WHITE
PLAINS

NEW YORK

NEW JERSEY

Fort
Washington

Fort
Lee

WESTCHESTER

Long Island Sound

Harlem
Heights

Hudson River

MANHATTAN
ISLAND

Kip's Bay

East River

CITY OF
NEW YORK

LONG ISLAND
(NEW YORK)

Brooklyn
Heights

THE NARROWS

STATEN
ISLAND

ATLANTIC OCEAN

John Glover

Over the summer of 1776, the British gathered a huge fighting force in and around New York City. General Howe, his brother Admiral Richard Howe, and Generals Clinton and Cornwallis jointly commanded a fleet of about three hundred ships and more than thirty thousand men. Continental soldiers and militiamen, under General Washington, numbered around nineteen thousand. On August 27, Generals Howe and Clinton landed fifteen thousand soldiers on Long Island and surprised Washington and about six thousand of his troops encamped on Brooklyn Heights. In heavy fighting, two thousand patriot fighters were killed, wounded, or taken prisoner. The inexperienced Americans found themselves trapped and close to defeat. Washington realized that escape was the only way to save the rest of his army. During the rain-soaked and foggy night of August 28, Colonel John Glover and his Marblehead Mariners—hardy sailing men from Massachusetts—used every available boat to ferry men and supplies across New York's East River to temporary safety in Manhattan.

Throughout the fall, New York was the scene of many conflicts. Battles were fought at Kip's Bay, Harlem Heights, and White Plains. Farther north, Benedict Arnold boldly challenged the British on Lake Champlain. Although his small fleet of gunboats and galleys couldn't defeat the powerful British naval force, his daring efforts caused the British to retreat to Canada for the winter instead of heading south to join General Gage. This was very good news for the Continental Army. In November, unsure of the next British move, Washington divided the army into three large forces—one group to defend Fort Washington in New York, another to guard Westchester, the gateway to New England, and a third to cross the Hudson River with him to Fort Lee, in New Jersey.

But on November 16, 1776, Fort Washington fell to the British, and almost three thousand patriot soldiers were taken prisoner. A few days later, as the British approached Fort Lee, Washington was forced to flee south to preserve the rest of his army.

British soldiers

German soldiers

British ships under fire from Fort Washington

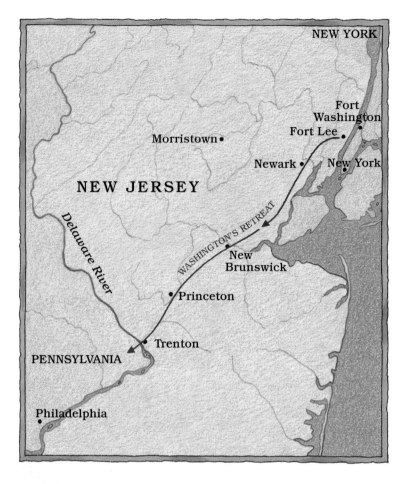

Cornwallis and his troops were hot on their heels as the Continental Army retreated through Newark, New Brunswick, and Trenton. On December 11, Washington's army crossed the Delaware River, using every boat they could find along the banks. After weeks of being on the run, the Continental Army escaped into Pennsylvania. From the relative safety of his new position, Washington had time to think. He knew that he had to turn the tide in favor of the Americans soon, or lose all hope of ever winning the Revolution. Thomas Paine, who had recently joined the army, wrote:

"These are the times that try men's souls. The summer soldier and sunshine patriot will, in this crisis, shrink from the service of their country; but he that stands it now, deserves the love and thanks of man and woman."

Paine's words were well timed. Many soldiers who were due to head home decided to stay and fight, and Pennsylvania militia rallied to the cause. Washington's army now stood at about six thousand men—barely enough to mount an attack against the British. But the general needed to make a bold move, and he felt that it was now or never.

An American spy brought Washington valuable information about the Hessian regiments housed in Trenton. Washington decided to carry out a surprise attack and catch these German soldiers off guard. On Christmas night, 1776, Colonel Glover and his Marbleheaders used a fleet of flat-bottomed boats to ferry three generals—Washington, Sullivan, and Greene—more than two thousand soldiers, and eighteen cannon across the Delaware.

It was a terrible night, and the weather made for tough going. Ice chunks floated in the river and the wind, sleet, and snow never let up. The crossings took nine hours, and it was almost dawn when they were all reassembled on the other side.

The crossing of the Delaware River

They marched the nine miles to Trenton and, at daybreak, took the Hessians totally by surprise. Most of the soldiers were still asleep after a long night of eating and drinking. In complete disarray, they fled in all directions as the Americans opened fire. In less than two hours, the Americans had achieved a stunning victory. More than nine hundred Germans were taken prisoner, and another hundred were killed or wounded. There had been no American losses! Exhausted, Washington and his army returned to Pennsylvania. As word of the victory spread throughout the colonies, the news was greeted with great joy. What a turnabout after such a difficult year! The British were amazed and furious—how had the ragtag Continental Army defeated such experienced and well-trained soldiers?

The battle at Trenton

Although they had won a victory, the Continental Army still suffered from lack of food and proper clothing. In a few days, almost half of the soldiers were again scheduled to leave for home. Washington pleaded with the men to stay, offering each a ten-dollar bounty for another six weeks. The men were more hopeful now and most agreed to stay. Within days, Washington led them back across the Delaware, looking for another chance to move against the British. They didn't have long to wait. General Cornwallis, in command of the British soldiers at Princeton, was on the march toward Trenton with more than seven thousand men. Arriving there, Cornwallis believed he had trapped Washington's army up against the river. Since it was almost dark, he decided to wait until morning to attack.

The Continental Army heads toward Princeton

Washington, however, had no intention of waiting for dawn. He would trick the British by taking off into the night and heading for Princeton to attack their remaining forces. Washington left enough men to keep the fires going and instructed them to make lots of noise, so that Cornwallis would believe the entire army was still encamped. Then they slipped quietly away, taking a back route to Princeton. When the advance guard, under General Hugh Mercer, met two British regiments, fierce fighting began. Washington rode into the thick of battle to rally his men. Together they charged the enemy until the British fled toward Trenton. Instead of following, Washington led his forces on to take Princeton and claim a second victory. Washington wanted to press on to New Brunswick to keep the British on their toes, but the winter weather was harsh and his men exhausted. So, reluctantly, he led the army to the winter headquarters in Morristown, New Jersey. The British defeats at Trenton and Princeton had raised everyone's spirits and given hope for the future of the Revolution.

King Louis XVI

Silas Deane

Arthur Lee

Although Congress was immensely pleased with Washington's victories, they knew that the Continental Army still had a long and difficult road ahead. The war was far from being won. Congress hoped to get the support of the French government in the fight against the British. With France as an ally, they stood a much better chance of success. So Congress sent Silas Deane, Arthur Lee, and Benjamin Franklin to ask the French for their support. For some time, France had secretly been sending small shipments of arms to the Americans. But if France were to openly side with the colonies, America would receive enough money and military support to win the war. And Washington's army was in dire need of help.

Living conditions at Morristown were extremely grim—the Continental Army barely survived the winter of 1777. Cramped in tiny huts in the freezing cold, without proper clothing to keep them warm, they struggled to fill their empty stomachs. Food rations were not enough to go around, and smallpox swept through the camp. Many men died and others deserted. Washington had only about three thousand soldiers left, most of them due to go home by the end of March. He begged Congress to approve funds for more men and supplies.

Morristown, New Jersey,
in the winter of 1777

In the meantime, the British were working out a grand plan to win the war. Ten thousand regulars, Loyalists, Canadians, and Indians, under Generals Burgoyne and St. Leger, would march south from Canada to take control of Lake Champlain and Fort Ticonderoga. Then they would move down the Hudson River to Albany, where they would be joined by General Howe and the rest of the British army. Together, they would take control of the river, separating New England and New York from the rest of the colonies. Divided, the colonies could never win the the revolution.

But by spring, things were looking up in the American camp. Washington's army had grown to about nine thousand, and weapons and ammunition had arrived from France—twelve thousand muskets! Washington needed to position his troops to be ready for a British attack. But it was hard to tell just what General Howe was up to. A number of times the British moved toward Philadelphia but then suddenly headed back to New York. So Washington split his army into five divisions to be ready for the British wherever they next appeared. His own division stayed in New Jersey to keep an eye on General Howe.

In the summer of 1777, General Burgoyne, known as "Gentleman Johnny," began to carry out the grand plan. Full of confidence, he marched south to Lake Champlain and Fort Ticonderoga. The Americans were ill-prepared to defend the fort. They had only about two thousand men—no match for Burgoyne's force of more than seven thousand. When the British positioned their cannon atop Mount Defiance, aimed directly at the fort, General Arthur St. Clair decided to abandon Ticonderoga. The Americans managed to escape, some on foot, others by boat, without having to surrender. They headed south toward Fort Edward.

John Burgoyne

British artillery aimed at Fort Ticonderoga

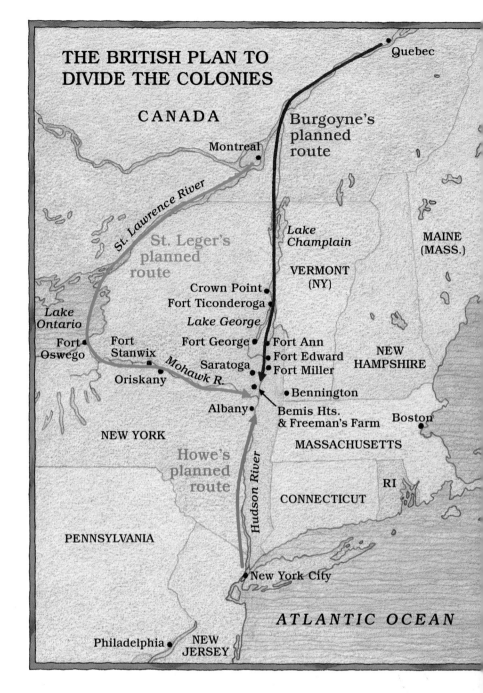

THE BRITISH PLAN TO DIVIDE THE COLONIES

Burgoyne marched south as well, and captured first Fort Anne and then Fort Edward, on the Hudson River. His army moved slowly, unused to the heavily wooded terrain. The fleeing patriot forces had destroyed bridges and littered the way with rocks and fallen trees. It took Burgoyne and his men almost a month to travel just twenty-five miles! Burgoyne was running low on supplies—he needed food and horses for his men. So he sent a force of Germans, Indians, and Loyalists to capture an American supply depot in Bennington, Vermont, about twenty-five miles away. There, his men were surrounded and attacked by almost two thousand Vermont and New Hampshire militiamen. When the Battle of Bennington ended, Burgoyne had lost more than a thousand men.

The success of the British plan depended on three armies coming together near Albany. But St. Leger had already abandoned the plan and turned back to Canada after he failed to seize Fort Stanwix near Oriskany, New York. Burgoyne decided to press on despite this setback. He hoped that General Howe's forces were on their way north to join him at Albany.

Morgan's sharpshooters attack the British at Bemis Heights

Horatio Gates

Daniel Morgan

Thirty miles north of Albany, near Saratoga, New York, the Northern Continental Army under General Horatio Gates blocked Burgoyne's way. Gates had fortified Bemis Heights above the Hudson and was encamped there with more than six thousand men, waiting for the British. On September 19, General Benedict Arnold, second in command, convinced a reluctant Gates to send Daniel Morgan's riflemen out to meet the advancing British at Freeman's Farm. When the fighting there grew fierce, Arnold took charge, bringing in his own regiments. His relentless strikes took a heavy toll until British reinforcements arrived. But General Gates failed to send in more men, and by nightfall Arnold was forced to retreat. Although victorious, the British lost six hundred men—twice the number of patriot losses.

For two weeks, there was little action. General Burgoyne waited, hoping for promised reinforcements. He desperately tried to hold out as his forces dwindled, his men dying from hunger and disease. Colonial forces, in the meantime, had almost doubled their numbers. On October 7, the British attacked and a second battle began. During an argument, Gates had relieved Arnold of his command. But Arnold ignored orders and rode out right into the middle of the action. Blind to the danger around him, his bravery inspired his fellow soldiers to fight harder. When he was hit by a musket ball in the leg, his horse shot out from under him, and Arnold was carried off the battlefield. But he had stirred the American army to victory.

The fierce battle left Burgoyne defeated, with seven hundred dead or wounded. By October 12, the British were out of supplies, short of men, and hemmed in with no possible means of escape. On October 17, 1777, they surrendered to General Gates. Burgoyne handed over his sword, and Saratoga was won.

Philadelphia

While Gates and Burgoyne faced off in New York, General Howe kept the rest of the Continental Army busy in Pennsylvania. He had chosen to take his army south, instead of going north to meet Burgoyne. In August, Howe had landed fifteen thousand men near Philadelphia, at about the same time that Washington and his army of twelve thousand had reached the capital. The Continental Army paraded through the city in a show of strength. A young French nobleman, the Marquis de Lafayette, rode at Washington's side. At Franklin's invitation, he had come from France to fight for the patriot cause. Washington immediately liked the nineteen-year-old soldier and asked him to serve as his aide.

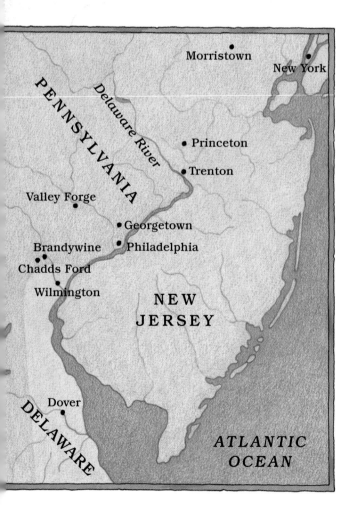

Marquis de Lafayette

Throughout September, Washington's army tried to prevent a British takeover of the capital. At the Battle of Brandywine, near Chadds Ford, they fought hard but suffered a costly defeat.

Massacre at Paoli, Pennsylvania, 1777

Congress quickly ordered reinforcements for Washington before fleeing Philadelphia for their own safety. Over the next few weeks, both armies camped outside the city, changing their locations several times. Small battles were fought at White Horse Tavern and Malvern Hill, and at Paoli, more than a hundred patriot soldiers were brutally massacred in a surprise bayonet attack. But despite Washington's efforts, on September 23, Cornwallis led British forces into Philadelphia to take control of the city.

In early October, Washington led an attack on the main British army under Howe at Germantown, just outside Philadelphia. A bold and elaborate plan to surprise the British was foiled by bad weather and bad luck. Soon after this defeat, the Americans also lost two valuable forts on the Delaware River. The British now had control of the Delaware, a major supply route to Philadelphia.

But as the year came to an end, there was good news to balance the bad. The French had learned of the amazing American victory at Saratoga, and now had more confidence in the future of the Revolution. They agreed to a formal alliance with the American colonies. It would take months to work out the details of the agreement, but the prospect of victory was now more likely. The beginning of 1778 found both armies encamped again for the winter months—Howe in Philadelphia and Washington at Valley Forge. Washington's men immediately began the most important task at hand—the construction of more than a thousand log huts. In the meantime, there were only tents for shelter. It was a terrible time for Washington and the Continental Army. Hunger was the most pressing problem—there simply was not enough food. Some days, the men had nothing but bread and water. Clothing was another problem. Many soldiers walked through the winter snows barefoot, for lack of shoes. The army was in grave danger of starvation and death from exposure to the cold. Washington pleaded with Congress for help, but he got no response.

General Washington writing to Congress

For much of the winter, Washington struggled to make his own arrangements for feeding and clothing his men. Lafayette felt so sorry for the soldiers that he sometimes used his own money to purchase what they needed.

The Marquis de Lafayette had come to America because he truly believed in the patriot cause. He was just nineteen and although he was a trained officer, he was very inexperienced. At first, he served as a volunteer at his own expense. But after Lafayette fought at Brandywine and Germantown, Washington asked Congress to put the Marquis in command of a division of Virginia troops. Lafayette was one of many European officers who came to America to fight for the ideals of liberty and freedom.

Winter at Valley Forge, 1778

In February, France and America agreed to two treaties of alliance. France officially recognized the independence of the colonies and pledged to help them win the war. The alliance meant that France was now at war with England as well. The British would be fighting two wars at once—one with the colonies and one with France. In March, they withdrew some of their forces in America to fight the French in the West Indies. General Henry Clinton was named commander of the British forces in America, replacing General Howe. All British soldiers in the American colonies were ordered back to New York City. They did not want to be trapped in Philadelphia if the French fleet arrived.

Von Steuben training the troops

This same winter, Baron Friedrich von Steuben came to Valley Forge. He had been an officer in the Prussian army and volunteered to instruct the troops in military drill, discipline, and use of the bayonet. All winter and into spring, von Steuben worked the soldiers relentlessly despite the dreadful conditions in camp. He spoke no English, so a translator gave his instructions to the men. The daily training sessions were exhausting but they raised the spirits of the soldiers. Lafayette, von Steuben, and Johann de Kalb, a Bavarian officer, helped the Continental Army survive that awful winter. Sadly though, because of the inaction of Congress, twenty-five hundred patriot soldiers perished at Valley Forge.

Baron von Steuben

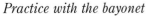
Practice with the bayonet

By May, the army was in much better shape—replacements had arrived, and food and clothing were more plentiful. When the troops marched in review for Washington's approval, he was most impressed. Von Steuben had truly transformed the Continental Army! Ignoring hardship, these disciplined, well-trained soldiers had come a very long way from the early days in Boston and New York.

A gun crew at practice

General Clinton had arrived in Philadelphia, and there were rumors that the British would soon be marching north, back to New York. Washington gave Lafayette command of an advance guard of several thousand men to keep an eye on the enemy. In June 1778, the British left Philadelphia, transporting troops, equipment, and many Loyalists to New York by land and by sea. Washington appointed Benedict Arnold as the military governor and commander of the continental forces in Philadelphia, and as soon as the British left, Arnold and his troops moved in.

As Clinton traveled north with the British army, Washington and the main body of the Continental Army followed closely behind them. On June 28, a few miles north of Monmouth Courthouse, New Jersey, Washington ordered General Charles Lee to lead an advance guard in an attack on Clinton's rear. When the Americans opened fire, the British turned to fight. Lee failed to properly take command, and gave confusing instructions to his men. Without leadership, the assault faltered and the soldiers retreated in disarray. At the sight of the fleeing troops, Washington became enraged. He dismissed Lee and took command himself, gathering his men and riding among them. He shouted words of encouragement, urging them on to battle. The soldiers quickly regained their confidence and began to defend against the British attack. In terrible heat, the Battle of Monmouth raged all afternoon, with many soldiers collapsing from exhaustion and sunstroke. Toward evening, the fighting finally stopped.

The Battle of Monmouth

Washington expected to resume battle at first light, but in the morning he discovered that Clinton and his army had slipped away during the night. The Americans felt victorious—they had held their own against the British in open combat. Both armies continued to march north toward New York City.

American Naval flags

The American Revolution was fought at sea as well as on land. British ships traveled the Atlantic shoreline, raiding and burning towns in New England and New Jersey. They sailed south to burn Portsmouth, Virginia, and attack Savannah, Georgia. The young Continental Navy wasn't big enough to attack the British fleet, but hundreds of small, privately owned ships were hired to bother and annoy British ships at sea. Across the Atlantic, a daring young captain, John Paul Jones, carried out a one-man rampage against the British navy in the waters around the British Isles.

The Americans hoped that the French navy would now help them to keep the British in check. In July 1778, a French fleet commanded by Admiral D'Estaing arrived at Newport, Rhode Island. Washington had expected the French navy to assist in American military operations, but each time plans were made something went wrong. In November, the French fleet sailed off to fight in the West Indies without a word to Washington.

John Paul Jones

Jones's ship, the Bonne Homme Richard, *battles the British ship* Serapis

The Revolution was also fought in the remote areas bordering the American colonies. Groups of Loyalists and Indians attacked towns and settlements in western New York and Pennsylvania, the Ohio Valley, and the mountains west of Virginia. Patriot forces under George Rogers Clark raided British forts and outposts in the wilderness of Indiana and the Illinois Territory. The British encouraged their Indian friends to terrorize settlers along the frontier. Near Albany, New York, Joseph Brant, a Mohawk chief, led bands of Iroquois on raids of villages and farms, killing frightened colonists. Washington ordered General Sullivan to stop the Iroquois, and American forces destroyed more than forty Indian towns, burning everything in sight. The Iroquois nation paid a terrible price for helping the British during the American Revolution.

Joseph Brant
(Thayendanegea)

An attack by British Loyalists and Indians on a colonial settlement

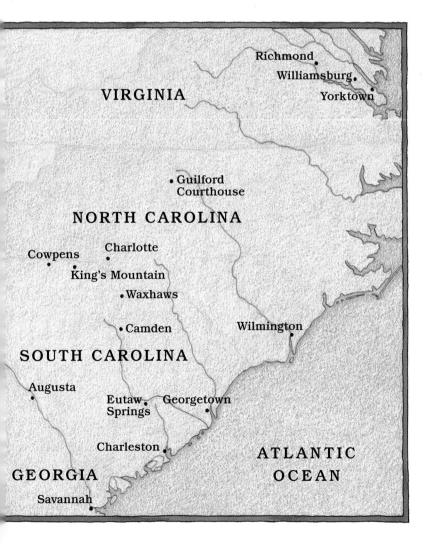

At the end of 1779, Washington's army returned to Morristown for the winter. General Clinton, instead, left New York with most of his army and sailed for Charleston, South Carolina. Earlier, the British had been victorious at Savannah, even though the colonial forces had help from the French fleet. The British now decided that the South was the place for them to win the war. With strong Loyalist support, they could defeat the patriots in the Carolinas and march on to Virginia and victory. With the arrival of Clinton's army, the British prepared to carry out their first step—the seizure of Charleston.

The Americans there were ready, but the numerous inlets, channels, and islands off the coast of Charleston made the city difficult to defend.

British bombs light up the sky above Charleston, South Carolina

The British landed on Johns Island, and then slowly crept closer to the city. In April 1780, they began a steady artillery bombardment of Charleston. After weeks of sleepless nights, the terrified residents begged General Benjamin Lincoln to surrender to the British. Losing Charleston was the biggest defeat of the war for the Americans—more than five thousand soldiers were taken prisoner.

Sir Henry Clinton

The Revolution was more than four years old, and everyone was weary of war. But with no victory in sight for either side, there was no choice but to keep on fighting. In the summer, General Cornwallis replaced Clinton as British commander in the South. At Camden, South Carolina, Cornwallis faced off against Gates. As usual, the American general left the running of the battle to others, and when the militia in the front row panicked and ran, the American lines collapsed. The British victory came with heavy losses for the patriot forces—only about seven hundred men survived out of more than four thousand. Shame was added to the bitter defeat: Gates fled from the battle scene and didn't stop till he was a good sixty miles away!

Lord Cornwallis

French naval officers and seamen

French soldiers

General Rochambeau

In the summer of 1780, another French fleet arrived in Newport with General Rochambeau, the new commander of all the French forces in America. He was ready to meet with Washington to map out a plan to defeat the British and win the war. But Washington needed time and money to build up his army again. His soldiers were all still suffering the ill effects of another terrible winter of cold and hunger. The men also had not been paid in a long while, and it was amazing that any had agreed to stay.

That fall, shocking news rocked the colonies: Benedict Arnold had turned traitor! It was almost impossible to believe. Arnold was a well-known American hero, but it seemed that he had become bitter about his lack of recognition and advancement in the army. During the years in Philadelphia, he had enjoyed a comfortable lifestyle, and had fallen in love with a young woman from a wealthy Loyalist family. It now appeared that he had helped the British get information about American military plans, and then had fled to England. He was soon appointed a brigadier general in the British army!

Meanwhile, in the Carolinas and Georgia, bands of patriot militia, led by courageous men like Francis Marion and Thomas Sumter, carried out bold and daring attacks against the British. Marion, known as the "Swamp Fox," would ride out with his men from hidden camps, deep in the bayou, to surprise the enemy in rapid, deadly assaults. However, the British had their own special warriors—Banastre Tarleton and Patrick Ferguson. Tarleton's legion of five hundred horsemen were swift in their pursuit of patriot forces, ruthlessly striking without mercy, sometimes killing men who had already surrendered. The British were victorious at Waxhaws, but the tide turned at King's Mountain, South Carolina, when Ferguson was killed and his Loyalist troops defeated.

Banastre Tarleton

Marion's men travel through the swamps by flatboat

After Camden, General Gates was a ruined man. Congress asked the commander in chief to choose a replacement. Washington's choice was General Nathanael Greene, an outstanding and loyal officer from Rhode Island. When Greene arrived in North Carolina, he quickly learned that in order to win in the South, he had to make good use of the militia, enlisting the aid of local men like Sumter, Marion, and "Light-Horse Harry" Lee, one of the best cavalry leaders of the Revolution. These men knew the countryside and had well-trained groups of fighters who were used to moving quickly. Greene also called on Daniel Morgan of Virginia, whose riflemen had played a big role at Saratoga. In no time, Morgan had Tarleton on his trail.

Nathanael Greene

Soldiers under Morgan's command

Delaware and Maryland continentals

Continental dragoon

Carolina and Virginia militiamen

On January 17, 1781, Morgan reached Cowpens, South Carolina, with about a thousand fighting men. During the night he came up with a detailed plan allowing each group of soldiers—infantry, riflemen, and militia—to do the job they were best at. When Tarleton arrived with eleven hundred men at dawn, Morgan set his plan into action, and in just over an hour the battle was won. Tarleton was defeated with most of his army dead, wounded, or captured. It was a much-needed victory for the Americans.

Throughout the fall and winter, Greene and Cornwallis chased each other's tails. There were battles at Guilford Courthouse, North Carolina, and at Eutaw Springs, South Carolina. Although the British won, they suffered very heavy losses. Throughout all the long months of war in the South, the Americans lost over and over again. But they never gave up. They kept fighting despite the failures and eventually began to wear the British out.

Washington and Rochambeau plan their next move

The year 1781 turned out to be the decisive year of the American Revolution. Just when everything was close to falling apart, many small events came together to bring the long war to a dramatic conclusion. The chain of events began in February, when General Washington ordered Lafayette and von Steuben to Virginia, with twelve hundred continentals, to repel a British raid led by Benedict Arnold. Then in April, unexpectedly, British general Cornwallis also headed for Virginia with his army of seven thousand. Later that spring, Rochambeau arrived in New York to meet with Washington. They were to plan their next move—an attempt to take New York City from the British.

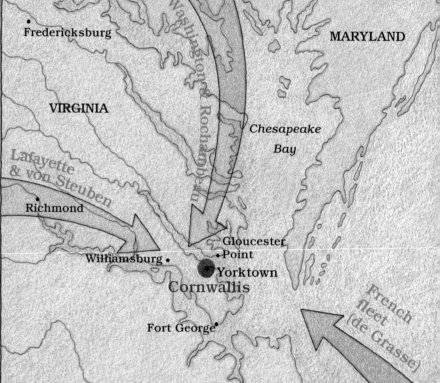

French soldiers digging trenches

A fife and drum corps in the British encampment

But in August, Washington and Rochambeau received two pieces of news: Cornwallis and his army were now encamped at Yorktown, Virginia, and Admiral de Grasse and his French fleet had left the West Indies, bound for the Virginia coast. Washington and Rochambeau quickly changed their plans and also headed for Virginia, marching south with their troops. The rest of the French fleet, anchored at Newport, now sailed for Virginia as well. Like the pieces of a giant puzzle, everything was falling into place.

By the beginning of September, de Grasse sailed into Chesapeake Bay with his fleet of ships. The French navy would prevent the British from landing reinforcements and equipment to aid Cornwallis. Within a few weeks, Washington and Rochambeau arrived in the capital of Williamsburg, near Yorktown, with their armies. The allied forces, including Virginia and Maryland militia, numbered about sixteen thousand men. Lafayette, Benjamin Lincoln, and von Steuben would each command a division of the American army, and the French commanders would take charge of their own troops. Washington, with the help of Rochambeau and de Grasse, would plan every move.

French fleet (from Newport)

ATLANTIC OCEAN

De Grasse's fleet forces British ships to return north

Admiral de Grasse

Cornwallis realized that he was in serious trouble. His army was trapped at Yorktown. He abandoned the outermost positions and retreated to temporary safety. He prayed that Clinton would soon send help by sea. On September 28, the allied forces marched toward Yorktown. They planned to besiege the British—pen them in, move closer and closer, pound them with cannon fire nonstop—then wait for them to give up. Since the British had no way out and supplies could not get in, it would be only a matter of time. By October 9, the bombardment began. Within a week, Cornwallis was desperate—he knew that he would have to surrender. On October 18, 1781, a red-coated drummer boy appeared atop a parapet, beating his drum to get the attention of the Americans and French. An officer emerged waving a white handkerchief, and at last the guns fell silent.

The British drummer boy

By evening, Cornwallis was forced to agree to an unconditional surrender. The next day at about eleven in the morning, the British officially surrendered at Yorktown. The American and French troops formed two lines, each a mile long, with Washington and Rochambeau at their heads. The British, except for Cornwallis, who claimed he was ill, marched by to throw down their arms. They looked only at the French. They were too angry and ashamed to face the Americans, the upstarts who had somehow defeated them. A British officer tried to present Cornwallis's sword to Rochambeau, who would not take it. Washington then directed General Lincoln to accept the sword on behalf of the Continental Army. It is said that on that day, the British musicians played a tune called "The World Turn'd Upside Down" until it was drowned out by the sounds of the now-American song, "Yankee Doodle." The war was over. The American Revolution was won.

The surrender at Yorktown

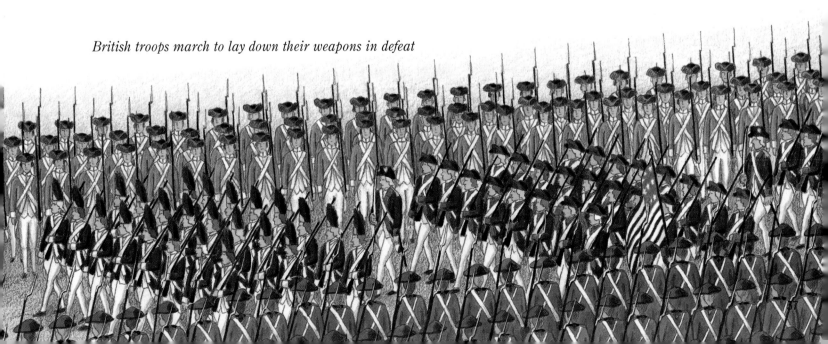

British troops march to lay down their weapons in defeat

When news of Yorktown reached Philadelphia, there was great joy and celebration. After more than six years, the war was over. But peace was not yet won. There was much more to be done. The years of war had left Congress without money to pay the army and no way to raise more. The huge task of creating a government for the new country lay before them. With British troops still in America, Washington had to keep his army together. But the soldiers wanted to go home, and they wanted to be paid. There was angry talk of rebellion and overthrowing Congress. Washington was greatly saddened. Had they gone through all these difficult years, only to throw it all away? He spoke to his men with great passion, pausing to put on his newly acquired glasses: "Gentlemen. You will permit me to put on my spectacles, for I have not only grown gray but almost blind in your service." Out of respect for their leader, the soldiers agreed to be patient a while longer.

Americans come out to greet and cheer General Washington

The official peace treaty between England and America was signed in 1783. British soldiers finally sailed for home. Great Britain recognized American independence and its new boundaries: Canada to the north, Florida to the south, and the Mississippi River to the west. George Washington said a sad farewell to his troops and officers, and then delivered his resignation to Congress. He asked the states—for they were no longer colonies—to help Congress bring them together as one country. The next few years would decide the fate of the new nation. The time of turmoil and worry would not be over until the young country made its way to steady ground. The nation's leaders and its people slowly realized how fortunate they were to have had Washington to lead them through the crisis of the war. Soon, they would call on him again to lead them to a lasting peace.

TABLE OF DATES

1763
End of the French and Indian Wars

1765
The Stamp Act passed

1770
The Boston Massacre

1773
The Boston Tea Party

1774
The First Continental Congress meets

1775
Paul Revere's Ride
Battles at Lexington and Concord
The Second Continental Congress meets
Washington takes command of the army
Battle of Bunker Hill (Breed's Hill)

1776
Paine's "Common Sense" published
British troops leave Boston for Canada
Declaration of Independence adopted
British fleet arrives in New York
Battle of Long Island
Forts Washington and Lee fall to the British
Washington's army retreats to Pennsylvania
Washington re-crosses the Delaware River
American victory at the Battle of Trenton

1777
Washington wins second victory at Princeton
Continental Army winters at Morristown
British troops invade from Canada
Fort Ticonderoga captured by British
Marquis de Lafayette arrives in America
British troops take over Philadelphia
American victory at Saratoga, New York
Continental Army winters at Valley Forge

1778
America and France agree on alliance
Baron von Steuben arrives at Valley Forge
British General Howe replaced by Clinton
British leave Philadelphia for New York
Americans re-take Philadelphia
Battle of Monmouth, New Jersey
British capture Savannah, Georgia

1779
John Paul Jones captures a British warship off the
    coast of England
Washington's army winters at Morristown

1780
British capture Charleston, South Carolina
Rochambeau arrives with a French fleet
Benedict Arnold discovered to be a traitor
American victory at King's Mountain
Nathanael Greene replaces Gates in the South

1781
American victory at Cowpens, South Carolina
Battle of Guilford Courthouse, North Carolina
General Cornwallis retreats to Yorktown
American and French forces arrive in Virginia
De Grasse arrives with French fleet
Americans besiege Yorktown
The British surrender at Yorktown

1782
Peace talks begin in Paris
Last battle of the war in the Ohio Territory

1783
Congress declares war over
British evacuate American cities
Loyalists leave America
Treaty of Paris officially ends the war
Washington resigns as commander in chief

UNSUNG HEROES OF THE AMERICAN REVOLUTION

These are a few of the true American heroes of the Revolution, men whose continuing contributions throughout the course of the war led to eventual victory. Although not as well known as leaders like Sam Adams, Patrick Henry, and John Hancock, each played a key role in the success of the patriot effort.

JOHN GLOVER (1732–1797) Born in Salem, Massachusetts, he later moved to Marblehead, where he became a fisherman and merchant shipowner. By 1776, he commanded the 14th Continental Regiment made up of fishermen and seafarers from Marblehead. Glover's Mariners fought with Washington in most of the early battles of the Revolution and twice saved the day for the Continental Army. In 1776, these brave and hearty soldiers evacuated Washington's army at the Battle of Long Island, and a few months later ferried that same army across the Delaware River on that famous Christmas night.

NATHANAEL GREENE (1742–1786) was born in Rhode Island and commissioned as a general in 1775. He served Washington throughout the Revolution and is considered by many to be the finest American general and military strategist of the war. As commander in the South, he directed the exhausting chase that led the British to retreat to Yorktown.

HENRY KNOX (1750–1806) was a bookseller in Boston and a member of the Massachusetts militia when Washington first made him colonel and then general in the Continental Army. He served as Washington's chief of artillery and was responsible for bringing Fort Ticonderoga's cannon to Boston in 1776. He served as a close advisor to Washington throughout the Revolution and was later appointed as the first secretary of war when Washington became president.

HENRY LEE (1756–1818) Born in Virginia and known as "Light-Horse Harry," he came to be known as the best cavalry officer of the Revolution. He was in charge of a special group of soldiers, called Lee's Legion. These men could fight on foot or on horseback with great speed and force. In the South, the Legion became one of the most outstanding units of the Continental Army, fighting in almost every battle in the region and doing much to bring about the British defeat.

FRANCIS MARION (1732–1795) commanded a brigade of one hundred and fifty fighters that lived in and fought from the marshes and waterways of South Carolina. British Commander Tarleton gave him the nickname the "Swamp Fox" because he was impossible to catch. Marion and his men harassed the British in daring raids, often disrupting their supply lines. His military skill brought about the important patriot victory at Eutaw Springs.

GEORGE MASON (1725–1792), a Virginian, served his country well during the years of the Revolution. His role is not as well known as the other heroes of the time, but his ideas and his writings greatly influenced the course of events. He wrote a draft constitution and bill of rights for Virginia that served as an inspiration to Jefferson when he wrote the Declaration of Independence and as a model for the national Bill of Rights, which would later become part of our Constitution.

DANIEL MORGAN (1736–1802) was born in New Jersey but settled in Virginia. In 1777, he was given the task of raising and commanding the company of Virginia riflemen who later played such an important role in the victory at Saratoga. Morgan was an excellent military strategist, and he led his riflemen to defeat the British at Cowpens. After the war, he represented Virginia as a congressman.

Hamilton East Public Library

BLACKS IN THE AMERICAN REVOLUTION

At the time of the Revolution, there were about 450,000 African American slaves in the colonies. In the conflict between the American colonists and the British, black Americans who were enslaved had no way of knowing how the outcome of the war would affect them. In New England, many joined the patriot cause, hoping that freedom for the colonists would also mean freedom for them. About 5,000 black soldiers, mostly from the North, fought on the patriot side during the war, both in the militia and in the Continental Army. In the South, the British offered slaves their freedom in exchange for service on their side. At the end of the war, about 20,000 black Loyalists left with the British. On both sides, many black soldiers fought bravely for what they thought was right without any guarantee of freedom or better living conditions at the end. The stories of most of these soldiers are undocumented, but there are a few whose stories are known.

Crispus Attucks, at the Boston Massacre, was the first American to die for the cause. **Peter Salem** was one of about twenty black militiamen who took up arms at Lexington and Concord. **Salem Poor** served bravely as a marksman at Bunker Hill, where some credit him with killing an important British officer. Later, he fought with the Continental Army in New York and wintered with them at Valley Forge. **James Armistead Lafayette**, a Virginia slave, served the Marquis de Lafayette as a spy. James volunteered as a waiter in Cornwallis's camp, reporting back to the Americans. After the war, he was awarded his freedom in payment for his valuable work, and he adopted the name of the Marquis as his own. Although the Revolution brought about freedom for some black Americans, particularly in the North, most African Americans continued to live in slavery.

WOMEN IN THE AMERICAN REVOLUTION

At the time of the American Revolution, women could not join the army to fight as soldiers. But women, young and old, contributed to the war effort in many ways on both sides, British and American. The roles played by individual patriot women were both large and small, but when taken as a whole, their service was vital to the success of the Revolution. Many of the active participants were the wives and daughters of soldiers and officers. These women often traveled with the army, nursing the sick and wounded and providing meals and clothing for the men. Sometimes, in emergency situations, they took up the arms of a wounded or dead loved one and fought in their place. Some brave females volunteered as spies or message runners. The women and girls left at home found themselves working twice as hard as before the war. They not only had all their usual chores and responsibilities, but they had to take over the jobs their husbands, brothers, and fathers had left behind. They worked farms, did manual labor, and ran businesses. Some women even turned their homes into hospitals to tend to the wounded.

Deborah Sampson joined the Continental Army in 1782 by pretending to be a man. She kept up her disguise for almost a year and a half before being discovered. She later received a military discharge and pension. **Margaret Cochran Corbin** fought beside her husband at Fort Washington, New York. When he was killed, she took over, loading and firing the cannon at the British until she was badly wounded. After the war, she was granted a disability pension by Congress. **Sybil Ludington** was the sixteen-year-old daughter of a colonel in the New York militia. When the British were approaching, she rode her horse more than forty miles at night to alert other local militiamen to the threat. **Lydia Darragh** was a Quaker housewife in Philadelphia. When the British used her house for a secret meeting, she managed to listen in on their plans. The next day, she found a way to bring the information to the American army, alerting them to a possible attack.

NATIVE AMERICANS AND THE AMERICAN REVOLUTION

In every conflict since the first Europeans reached the shores of North America, including the American Revolution, the only group of people who always lost out were the first Americans. Native American groups in the eastern half of the continent tried hard to retain their lands and way of life. But as the European explorers and settlers became permanent residents, they took more and more away from Native Americans. Some tribes or nations made alliances with the British, the French, and the new Americans in hopes of preserving something of their land and customs. But most of the time their trust was betrayed by their so-called allies, and they found themselves worse off than before. During the Revolution, many tribes tried to be neutral. Some joined the British, hoping for land protection, while others fought for the patriot cause. They served in militias in New England and later in the South as well. But in Iroquois country and on the western frontier, although loyalties were split, Americans generally regarded all Indians as enemies who were allied with the British. Many Indians and American settlers lost their lives in the fighting. In the end, when the peace treaties were signed, neither the British nor the Americans made any attempt to save Indian land from settlement. The new nation would prove to have little regard for the first settlers of North America. The interests of Native Americans were never protected as promised, and their plight only grew worse after the Revolution.

MORE ABOUT THE AMERICAN REVOLUTION

Population In the year 1760, there were about 1,610,000 people living in the American colonies. By 1780, the population had grown to about 2,781,000. Over the eight years of war, almost 232,000 men served in the Continental Army. At least another 160,000 served in local militias. More than 4,400 Americans died fighting and more than 6,000 were wounded in battle.

The Articles of Confederation The Articles of Confederation were adopted by the Continental Congress in 1781. These articles served as the first constitution, or rules of government. Before this, each colony had its own government, but with the fight for independence came the need for one central government. The Articles served this purpose until the present Constitution was adopted in 1788.

Haym Salomon Haym Salomon was born in Poland and arrived in New York City just before the Revolution. He was a Jewish merchant who spoke a number of languages, including German. He believed in the patriot cause and began to work as a spy, supplying the American army with information about Hessian activity. He was arrested several times and condemned to death but managed to escape and flee to Philadelphia. There, he became a successful banker. Over the years, he lent most of his money to the American government to pay for the war. He died a poor man at the age of forty-five. The American government owed him about $650,000, which they never repaid.

Nathan Hale Nathan Hale was an American spy who gave his life for his country. He was born and raised in Connecticut and graduated from Yale College in 1775. He joined the Continental Army and served under George Washington in New York. He volunteered to spy on the British behind enemy lines. Disguised as a schoolmaster, he was captured with evidence that he had been spying for the Americans. He was executed by hanging the very next day, at the age of twenty-one. He is most famous for his last words: "I only regret that I have but one life to lose for my country."

George Rogers Clark George Rogers Clark was born in Virginia in 1752. He was commissioned as a major in the Virginia militia in 1777. His mission was to end British control in the western frontier areas. He organized a force of soldiers and led them on raids of British forts and settlements in the Illinois Territory. He was aided by the many French settlers of this area who hated the British and had learned of the American-French alliance. Even though Clark and his forces gained control of many British settlements, the biggest prize—the fort at Detroit—remained firmly in British hands until the settlement of the war.

Colonial Life Despite the war, life went on in the colonies. The first medical school, the first planetarium, and the first theater opened in Philadelphia. Chocolate was manufactured in the colonies for the first time, and the first daily newspaper began printing. The North and South linked their postal systems with regular monthly boat trips between South Carolina and New York. The first official American flag was made in 1775 and replaced in 1777 with the first version of the red, white, and blue stars and stripes.

Exploration Exploration and settlement continued away from the East Coast colonies. Daniel Boone made his first trip beyond the Appalachian Mountains, and in 1769 he traveled through the Cumberland Gap into Kentucky Territory. In 1775, he established the settlement of Boonesborough along the Kentucky River. On the other side of the continent, Spanish priests were exploring parts of California. Father Junipero Serra established a mission settlement near what is now San Diego. In 1776, another mission was established farther north, near present-day San Francisco.

John Paul Jones and the American Navy Though at the time of the American Revolution the American Navy was tiny and not up to defending our shores in battle, there was reason to take pride in one naval hero. John Paul Jones, who was commissioned as a captain in the American Navy, used his ships to raid British ports and daringly attack British ships in European waters. Given control of a number of French ships, Jones captured seventeen British vessels. His most famous battle at sea was his capture of the British flagship, *Serapis*, in 1779.

The First Submarine In September 1776, the first working submarine was launched in New York Harbor in an attempt to sink a British ship. This first submarine, called *The Turtle*, was invented and built by David Bushnell near Old Saybrook, Connecticut. It was piloted by Ezra Lee of Old Lyme, Connecticut, who had to operate the vessel single-handedly. Even though the mission failed, it was the first use of a submarine in naval combat.

The Declaration of Independence Fifty-six members of Congress from all thirteen colonies signed the Declaration of Independence. Almost half the men were lawyers or judges. Many were merchants, gentlemen farmers, and plantation owners. They all agreed to sign this important document even though they risked their lives to do so. Most suffered personal loss of some kind during the war. Two of the signers became presidents of the new nation—Thomas Jefferson and John Adams. They died on the same day, July 4, 1826, exactly fifty years after the signing.

INDEX